A BOOK OF HOPE
after Retirement

THE BEST YEARS ARE AHEAD

*written by...*Dr. Robert Hill, PHD   *edited by...*Cecil O. Kemp, Jr.

written by ...
Dr. Robert Hill, PHD

A very, very special thanks to ...
Stephen von Hagel, Robert Kiefer and Brenda McClearen. Stephen had the idea for The Hope Collection and shepherded the creative effort, working closely with Robert, Brenda and their associates.

edited by ...
Cecil O. Kemp, Jr.

Art Direction ...
McClearen Design Studios
3901 Brush Hill Rd.   Nashville, TN 37216   615-859-4550

To Reach the Author and Publisher ...
The Wisdom Company, Inc.
P. O. Box 681351   Franklin, TN 37068-1351
1-615-791-7186

Copyright 1999, by The Wisdom Company, Inc., Nashville, Tennessee.
ISBN# 1-893668-03-7

All rights reserved. No portion of the book may be copied without written permission of The Wisdom Company, Inc., except when used in a critical review. Published in the United States of America by The Wisdom Company, Inc.

About The Hope Collection –

Each Hope Collection book is based on Cecil O. Kemp, Jr's acclaimed inspirational book, **Wisdom Honor & Hope**.

Hope—without it, no one can live very long.

No great conquests have ever been won without it.

No one has ever seen better days without hoping for them.

Nurture hope and it will reward you.

Hope is the sunshine of life and the angel that puts a song in your heart.

What gives you hope?

The authors and publishers invite you to enjoy this and other Hope Collection Gift Books.

About the Creator of The Hope Collection –

Cecil O. Kemp, Jr. lived his dream, becoming a successful businessman and business owner. Yet, he was very unfulfilled. Enormous material success didn't deliver on its promises of hope and happiness. He set out to discover the secrets of a genuinely happy, hopeful life. Finding and applying them, he freed himself and his family from the rat race life, while enjoying even greater material success. After nearly two decades of this higher prosperity, he offers those amazing discoveries in The Hope Collection. Kemp and other Hope Collection writers invite readers to begin their own journey of the heart toward real and lasting peace, hope, happiness and success.

Introduction

Recent studies reveal that few people are adequately prepared for the inevitable transition to the Golden Years of life. The Golden Years can be the most happy, productive, and fulfilling part of our lives, depending on the choices we make. This book has been written especially for people who are entering their Golden Years to help them discover the possibilities of this prime time of life.

Each of the book's four convenient sections deals with one primary aspect of life in the Golden Years: emotional, physical, financial, and spiritual. You may read the whole book at one sitting, read one part at a time, or read one topic each week. However you approach your reading, we believe when you read the book and apply the principles of Wisdom, you can make your Golden Years the most happy and prosperous of your lifetime.

In his book Wisdom Honor & Hope, Cecil O. Kemp, Jr., shares this wisdom: Our life is currency we get to spend only once. Living a happy and truly fulfilled life is achieved living it wisely. There is always a best way to do everything. The greatest human power is choice. Real and lasting success is found choosing to travel the Path of Wisdom, Honor, and Hope.

The Prophet Jeremiah wrote, speaking of God's plans for us to travel the path of life, For I know the plans I have for you. They are plans for good...to give you a future and a hope.

Come with me and consider the best way to live the Golden Years, traveling that path.

—*Bob Hill*

The best is yet to be,
The last of life, for which the first was made;
Our times are in His hand, Who saith, A whole I planned,
Youth shows but half; trust God, see all, nor be afraid.
–*Robert Browning*

PART ONE

your *Emotional Transition*

Far away there in the sunshine are my highest aspirations. I may not reach them, but I can look up and

see their beauty,

believe in them, and try to follow where they lead.

—Louisa May Alcott

Landmarks

...that you may prosper in all things, and be in health as your soul prospers.
—St. John

Every life has landmarks. Landmarks are the turning points in our lives that teach and change us. They can be positive or negative; they can mark the birthplace of wise or unwise habits. All inner landmarks, directly or indirectly, influence our past, present, and future behavior-including how we adjust our daily attitudes. Beginning your Golden Years is a significant landmark. By walking in the ways of Wisdom, you can choose to make this landmark a wonderful, hopeful, and happy turning point in your life.

Nugget of Hope

Our life is a self-portrait of the philosophy and habits we choose to live by. —Cecil O. Kemp, Jr.

Words

as we *think*
in our *heart,*
so are we. —King Solomon

*As we think
in our heart,
so are we
—King Solomon*

Most long-lived people are also loving people-generous, kind, and unselfish. We are loving people when we accept other people the way they are without criticizing or judging them, or trying to manipulate or change them. Cecil O. Kemp, Jr., in his book *Wisdom Honor & Hope*, says that words are a power unto themselves. To assure harmony and achieve excellence in relationships, he advises always using soft, gentle, and kind words-what he calls powderpuff words. Dr. Solomonovich, a Russian gerontologist who spent long periods living in close proximity with the long-lived Abkhasian people in the Caucasus, reported that he had never heard any of the long-lifers use harsh words. They have learned the value of using powderpuff words.

Nugget of Hope
To keep the heart unwrinkled, to be hopeful, kindly, cheerful, reverent-that is to triumph over old age.
—Thomas Bailey Aldrich

your Thoughts

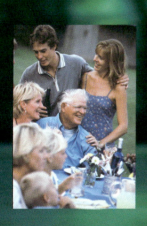

*Whatever is true, honest,
just, pure, lovely and good,
think on these things.*
—*St. Paul*

Most people agree that a positive mindset can influence the body in positive ways. Our heart-held spiritual beliefs, principles, and values are the building blocks of our thoughts, thinking, and mindset, according to Cecil O. Kemp, Jr. He observed that a spiritually wise heart is critical to healthy emotions, thoughts, and attitudes,

and to physical health.

There is overwhelming evidence that the mind can heal. On the other hand, diseases are more likely to attack those whose mindset is negative. Continued negative thoughts result in depression, allowing toxins to be released into our physical systems. We can avoid and overcome many cases of depression by controlling our thoughts. Wisdom leads us to let our minds be guided by our wise, honorable, and hopeful hearts.

Nugget of Hope
How things look on the outside of us depends on how things are on the inside of us. —Parks Cousins

Self Image

Depend on what is inside you, **not what is outside.**—Cecil O. Kemp, Jr.

You will find in your Golden Years the perfect time to think about your strengths and to let yourself be forgiven for your weaknesses. You can feel confident and optimistic about the future if you adopt a positive mindset. When you feel good about yourself, you will feel good about other people and about life itself. Take advantage of the Golden Years to revisit your attitude about competing with other people. Keeping up with the Joneses is a continual drain on your emotions and energy that you can remove from your life. Excel at something, then compete only with your own excellence. You will be energized!

Take advantage of the
Golden Years

Nugget of **Hope**

No one can make

you feel inferior
without your consent.

—*Eleanor Roosevelt*

You will be
energized

Self Worth

Grow in grace and knowledge of our Lord. —St. Peter

Most of us have the overwhelming and continuing desire to feel productive and useful. These needs remain important in the Golden Years. According to Abraham Maslow's Hierarchy of Needs, they are necessary for our self worth and to give us reasons for living. Maslow lists self-actualization—developing one's fullest capacity and finding meaning in life—as the highest order of needs. He sees esteem needs—a sense of adequacy, competence, achievement, contribution, or recognition and prestige—as the second highest order of needs.

When we live according to the principles of Wisdom, we find ways to be productive and useful to others at any time of our lives. In our Golden Years, we can continue to succeed by putting the needs of others above our own.

Nugget of **Hope**
For age is opportunity no less than youth itself.
—Henry Wadsworth Longfellow

Attitude

This is the day that the Lord has made;
we will *rejoice* and *be glad* in it.
—King David

Fear, anxiety, and worry are deadly killers that make it easier to get all kinds of disease and effectively destroy the quality of life we deserve in our Golden Years. The opposite of fear and worry is faith and trust.

Dr. Norman Vincent Peale said that we tend to get what we expect. If you paint in your mind a picture of bright and happy expectations, you put yourself into a condition conducive to your goal. To have that state of mind, take time to develop a strong belief and faith in God, in yourself, in life, and in the fellow travelers that come your way. People with an honest faith are rarely disappointed.

If we dwell on the things we fear, they are sure to come to pass, according to an ancient homily. So, look today squarely in the face and resolve that you will face it without fear, worry, or anxiety. It is the day which the Lord has made. Therefore, we may rejoice and be glad in it. A positive mindset can escort your fears to flight!

faith & trus

Nugget of Hope
I am convinced that life is 10% what happens to me and 90% how I react to it.
—Charles Swindoll

MIND & BRAIN

Mind

One of the first things people must do to be successful is to **quit their stinkin' thinkin'.**
—Zig Ziglar

William James, one of the most widely read nineteenth-century philosophers, concluded that the greatest discovery of his generation was the fact that human beings can alter their lives by altering the attitudes of the mind. This remains true for us, today.

As we approach our Golden Years, we can change our lives for the better by learning to
- Check every negative thought;
- Recognize what negative thinking does to us;
- Think of positive alternatives and outcomes; and
- Replace each negative thought with a positive statement.

"And remember," Jesus said,

"everything is possible for the person who truly believes."

● Nugget of Hope

Our duty is making ourselves a product of God within us, beginning with attaining a spiritually wise heart.
—*Cecil O. Kemp, Jr.*

Habits

As the twig is bent, so the tree is inclined.

—Virgil

Habits are behavior patterns that grow out of our thinking (in the heart first), and then, doing or not doing something in the same way, over and over again, for a period of time. Philosopher Earl Nightingale wrote that we become what our most dominant thoughts are.

Through action or inaction, we become whatever our most dominant heart thoughts are, since these determine our habits.

Our lives and destinies depend heavily on the thought patterns from which our habits grow.

First, we can pattern our mindsets and our heart-thoughts toward Wisdom. Then, we will naturally choose to adopt wise habits that will become a positive part of our characters.

Nugget of Hope
Habit can be your best servant or your worst nightmare, depending on whether its source is a wise or unwise heart.
—Cecil O. Kemp, Jr.

Forgiveness

Be kind to one another, tenderhearted, forgiving one another, even as God in Christ forgave you.

—St. Paul

Anger, bitterness, hostility, and resentment will drive happiness and health from our lives. Hostile people have cardiovascular disease five times more often than those who are loving. Even though the Golden Years can be a wonderful time of life, some older people are cantankerous and mean, angry at the world. Perhaps they need to seek and to give forgiveness.

The opposite of anger and resentment is love and forgiveness. We can find joy in forgiving, now and always, those we believe may have caused us any harm. By forgiving others, we release bitterness from our lives, treat ourselves to happiness, and adopt a loving attitude. Remember, as Cecil O. Kemp, Jr., wrote in *Wisdom Honor & Hope*, forgiving is one of the most important principles of Wisdom. It is the first principle and value, to resolve conflicts and begin personal and relationship healing.

Nugget of Hope
The best part of health is a fine disposition.
—*Ralph Waldo Emerson*

Laughter

A merry heart does good like a medicine, but a broken spirit dries the bones. —King Solomon

Few long-lifers take themselves too seriously. They laugh often at themselves and their mistakes. They maintain a youthful enthusiasm for anything new and different. And they possess an almost childlike enthusiasm for spontaneous fun and play.

We can choose to add fun and laughter to our lives, no matter what the circumstances. Some years ago, writer and editor Norman Cousins was diagnosed with a serious auto-immune disease for which there was no certain cure. Cousins was aware of the therapeutic benefits of fun and laughter, so he asked that his treatment include regular doses of Three Stooges, Marx Brothers, and Abbott and Costello movies. Much to the surprise of his doctors, Cousins's pain was alleviated to a great extent during the time he was laughing.

Eventually, he recovered completely. The therapeutic benefits of laughter were undeniable in his case.

Our lives and our health can improve when we remember to laugh and be joyful.

Nugget of Hope
Remember this—that very little is needed to make a happy life.
—*Marcus Aurelius*

Staying Active

They shall be *fresh and flourishing.*
—King David

Active

The secret to longevity can be summed up as living the good life. When we retire, we go on living-we just change our occupations. Instead of devoting our energy to the daily grind, we finally have time to explore new possibilities. Learn to paint, listen to music, read an epic poem, seek the beauty of nature. There are hundreds of challenging occupational life-extenders that can help us to live well and live happy. When we choose to stay active in some way, we refresh and revitalize our lives.

Nugget of Hope
[Life] abounds with pleasure if you know how to use it. —*Seneca*

Generosity

> *Give and it shall be given unto you.*
> —*St. Paul*

Most Golden Agers have experience, or time, or money, or specific expertise that younger people may not. This is the time to be generous! Many people would be grateful for your time, just to talk, or to help them get through a difficulty. Your life experience qualifies you to help others with expert advice on the problems of living. Being generous with your accumulated wisdom in this way is spiritually fulfilling and uniquely satisfying. This is also a time to be generous with your money. Wisdom tells us that misers hoard their treasure and reap misery. Givers give generously without thought of return—and reap a harvest of love.

Nugget of Hope
We reap a harvest from the seeds we sow. Sow generously.
—Cecil O. Kemp, Jr.

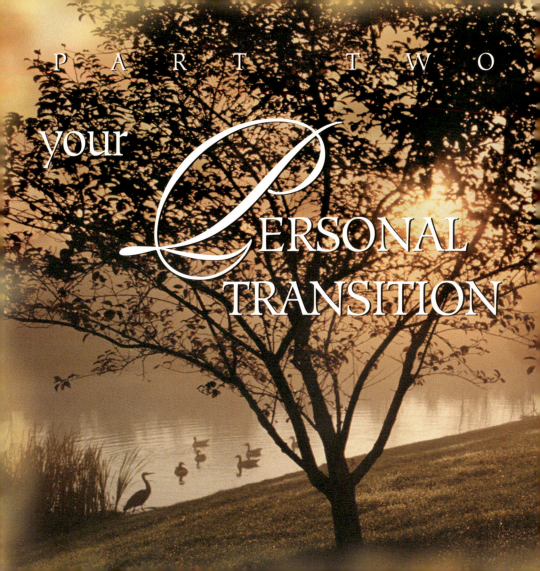

Aging

I pray that you will prosper in all things and be in health, *just as your soul prospers.*

—St. John

We can't turn back the clock, but we can choose our attitudes toward aging. Aging can be measured in three ways:

- biological or chronological aging, a process that can be slowed by an effective exercise program and a nutritious diet;
- psychological aging, related to behavior and/or reactions to increasing biological age—we become as old as we think we are;
- social aging, or how we react to a changing society; we can choose to think young when we let ourselves be guided by Hope for the future.

Applying the principles of Wisdom to our lives, and taking responsibility for our aging process, can help us stay young at heart!

Nugget of Hope
One cannot avoid growing older, but one does not have to become old.

Lifespan

And even to gray hairs, God will carry you.

—*Isaiah*

Our bodies were created to last a lifetime. But how long is a lifetime? That may depend on you!

Within a generation or two, the maximum human life span of about 120 years could be extended by decades. What condition your spirit and body will be in thirty, forty, or even fifty years from now will be significantly affected by your actions today. A nutritious diet, adequate rest, a calm approach to the vicissitudes of life, and giving love generously can all affect your lifespan.

Remember, King David said, "Teach us to number our days, realize how few they are, and spend them wisely."

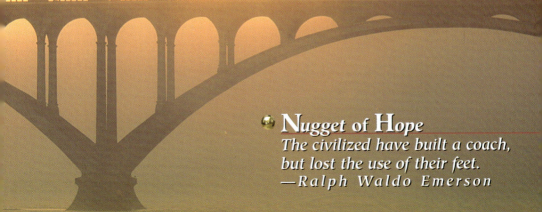

Nugget of Hope
The civilized have built a coach, but lost the use of their feet.
—Ralph Waldo Emerson

Quality of Life

May your spirit, soul, and body be kept strong and blameless until that day the Lord comes back again.
—St. Paul

If you live to be sixty-five years of age, the chances are good that you will live at least twenty more years. The quality of life in your later years depends upon your present inner and outer lifestyle.

Noted author Dean Kelley wrote, "A tree will keep on growing so long as it continues to get food, water, and sun." He reminds us that it may not grow any larger, but it will continue to grow and produce so long as it gets adequate sustenance.

Humans need food, water, and sun, just as the tree needs them. We also need to feed our spirits by living wisely and with appreciation for the many gifts God has given us. Then our life quality will truly shine from within.

Nugget of Hope
Some feel old at 40, while others feel young at 75.

Your Body

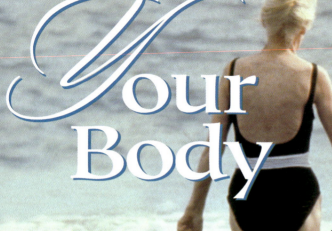

Be watchful and **strengthen** *the* **things** *which* **remain.**

—*Jesus*

The workings of the human body are intricate and interdependent. Every part of your body works with every other part. To keep your body working harmoniously, you must keep it in the best possible condition.

In his book, *The Psychology of Aging*, Dr. James Birren notes that decline in active exercise usually begins at about age forty, but this does not necessarily apply. We can choose to remain active, at whatever level is possible, for as long as we live.

Nugget of Hope
Become aerobically fit, and fat (weight) will take care of itself.
—*Covert Bailey*

Exercise

Everyone who **competes in the games** *goes into strict training.*
—St. Paul

The importance of regular exercise cannot be overly stressed. It affects every area of our being, including our spirit and our attitude toward life.

Consider your nervous system, particularly critical to aging. Blood circulation to the brain affects many of the processes of aging. Lack of circulation can damage the nervous system and hasten aging, because, unlike many other organs of the body, the nerves cannot regenerate.

Even moderate exercise can improve circulation—and help the rest of our body systems to stay in tip—top condition, as well. Let's exercise our bodies to keep them fit!

Nugget of Hope
Walking is the best medicine.
—Hippocrates

Nutrition

And the Lord God made all kinds of trees that were pleasing to the eye and good for food.
—Moses

Appropriate nutrition for the body is still possible to achieve, even in our fast-paced society where junk food has become the norm for most families. Golden Agers can model a wise diet for their families, and help arrest the aging process at the same time.

It's never too late to learn the art of healthful grocery shopping, often referred to as round-the-wall shopping. In most grocery stores, the breads, fresh fruits and vegetables, and dairy products are usually stocked around the four walls of the store. The inside aisles are full of processed foods, many of which are very expensive and not very nutritious. Shop round-the-walls, and you will automatically make wiser food choices. And, just for good measure, look at the nutrition label on every food product you buy. The label helps you make sure you're getting nutritional bang for your buck.

Nugget of Hope
Some people may be stressed because of "stressed" spelled backwards.

t were pleasing to the eye and good for food.

Delaying Aging

But one thing I do: Forgetting what is behind, **I work for the prize that is ahead.**

—St. Paul

Aging can be delayed by a plentiful diet, regular sleep and short naps, and moderate exercise. This modern-sounding advice, with which most of today's health professionals would agree, was written more than 350 years ago by Sir Francis Bacon, in his book *History of Life and Death*! Such good advice has stood the test of time and still applies as we approach the twenty-first century.

While a decline in exercise is considered normal as we mature, the sooner we stop exercising, the more rapidly we age. Conversely, eating well, keeping our sleeping habits regular, and exercising moderately can delay the aging process considerably.

🥮 Nugget of Hope
The best preparation for tomorrow is to do today's work superbly well.
—Sir William Osler

Exercising the Mind and Brain

Until I come, *give attention to reading.*
—St. Paul

We've all heard the saying, "You can't teach an old dog new tricks." That may be true for canines, but it is definitely not true for people! Your mind can remain sharp in your Golden Years, and your knowledge can continue to grow.

Education knowledge is gained through study. Wisdom knowledge is gained by experience, and, the older we become, the more experiences we accumulate. Life experiences, pleasant and unpleasant, could be termed exercise for the brain. You can keep your spirit and your mind healthy and growing by reading the Bible daily and by reading wholesome books and newspapers regularly. Carefully chosen radio and television programs and movies can also keep the spirit and mind stimulated. Share what you learn with your friends and your family. Let the exercise of experience clean out the cobwebs in your mind!

Nugget of Hope
Reading is to the mind what exercise is to the body.

Appearance

> *I am like a groom in his wedding suit or a **bride with her jewels.***
> —The Prophet Isaiah

Have you ever had a "bad hair day"? Some people mistakenly think that the Golden Years are just one bad hair day after another. There are two keys to keeping your appearance at its best as you age: the outside and the inside.

If your old suit or dress is still in good condition and in style, why not continue to wear it? If you choose new clothes, find classic styles that suit your age and personality. They need not be expensive. You'll face each day with a smile when you bathe, comb your hair, and dress neatly, whether or not you plan to go out.

Most important, tend to the values and principles of Wisdom. What really counts is what is in our hearts, and our "outsides" reflect our "insides." The most beautiful clothing and the most careful grooming gain significance only from a beautiful spirit.

Nugget of Hope
You never get a second chance to make a first impression.

Adjusting Habits

Everything may be permissible to me, but I will not be mastered by anything. —St. Paul

By the time we reach our Golden Years, we have probably adopted several habits, some wise and some unwise. Unwise habits may endanger the length as well as the quality of our lives. Happily, we can learn to recognize and adjust our unwise habits in time to delay or reverse some of the aging processes.

Consider the three Ds:

- **Desire**—This means we really want to adjust our unwise habits.
- **Determination**—This shows we are willing to put some effort into changing for the better.
- **Discipline**—This means we have made a heart commitment to take responsibility for our habits, even when our minds and bodies rebel.

We can choose to change our unwise habits into wise habits by following the heart-held beliefs, principles, and values of Wisdom.

⁕ Nugget of Hope
Don't put off for tomorrow what you can do today.
—James A. Michener

Lifestyle

I don't understand myself at all, for I really want to do what is right.

—St. Paul

Sometimes our lifestyles don't really reflect our heart-held beliefs and principles. Perhaps we have let unwise habits point our lifestyles in the direction of Folly. It is never too late to begin to adjust our lifestyles in positive and fruitful ways. So, start today!

Begin to think of others' needs ahead of your own. Hold yourself accountable for your decisions. Concentrate on the people and activities in your life that are really important. Choose an attitude of cooperation, love, and integrity. You will be amazed at how quickly you can adjust to a new, hopeful, healthy lifestyle when your heart is guided by Wisdom.

Nugget of **Hope**
Success is more attitude than aptitude.

Sex in Your Golden Years

And God created them man and woman.
—*Moses*

God created us as sexual persons. In spite of the widely held misconception that Golden Agers are no longer interested in sex, most recent studies reveal that people continue to enjoy sex well into their seventies and even their eighties.

Many older people have not spoken openly about sex in the past, partly because sex may have been considered a socially unacceptable, completely private topic. Nowadays, many of us are more comfortable with seeking solutions to problems such as impotence and discomfort, since such conditions can often be treated successfully. Some recent studies even claim that weekly sex may be a deterrent to arthritis!

Sex in the Golden Years can be a beautiful, God-given way to express gentleness, patience, kindness, faithfulness, self-control, and unconditional love—qualities of grace that are born in the ageless, Spirit-led heart.

Nugget of Hope
There may be snow on the roof, but there is fire on the hearth.

PART THREE

your Financial Transition

Inner spirituality and peace is the first priority of those who want to be truly successful with their life and money. Applying the principles and values of Wisdom is the only way to manage your life and money—if you want both to count for what really counts.

—Cecil O. Kemp, Jr.
(author of Wisdom & Money,
The Laws Of Highest Prosperity)

Assessing Needs

Only the foolish do not financially prepare; they must eat the fruit of their behavior.

— Cecil O. Kemp, Jr.

Can you be assured, after you retire, that all your financial needs will be met for the rest of your life? That's difficult to predict. But you can prepare financially for retirement to the best of your ability and knowledge. Much of the frustration and anxiety we experience with financial matters comes from lack of preparation.

Most financial planners believe that you will need about 80 percent of your present income to continue the lifestyle you are now living, provided your home is clear of debt.

Cecil O. Kemp, Jr., in his book *Wisdom and Money*, wrote, "Be safe, not sorry. Plan on needing 100 percent of your pre-retirement income. I have never met retirees who were unhappy they had saved too much money for their Golden Years....Remember wise King Solomon's advice about preparation. He said, 'Go to the ant. Consider her ways and be wise: She has no guide, overseer, or ruler, but she prepares and saves in the summer, so she will have food for the winter.'"

Careful planning is a wise choice.

Nugget of Hope

Tomorrow's comforts demand today's priorities.
—*Merrill Lynch*

Credit Cards

For best results with money, consider these wise rules of spending:

(1) Budget spending last!
(2) Avoid buying on credit.
(3) Never buy on impulse.
(4) Buy at the right time. Timing matters!
(5) Brand name, convenience, and first class are not essential!

—Cecil O. Kemp, Jr.

Consumer debt is at an all time high and spending has reached epidemic proportions, according to many economists. Most people have used credit cards for impulse buying and are paying dearly for items they thought they wanted, but didn't really need. The average family in the U.S. today spends more than 22 percent of its income as interest on debt.

A comfortable retirement cannot be based on consumer debt. As we get older, we can choose to pay off our credit cards and use them only for emergencies. If we use them at all, we can be sure to pay the balance in full at the end of each month.

As Cecil O. Kemp, Jr. points out in his book *Wisdom & Money,* research indicates that people who don't use credit spend 25 percent less than those who do. The after-tax return on a dollar invested to pay off a dollar owed on a credit card is normally between 18 and 25 percent—a very respectable yield!

Nugget of Hope

A good pair of scissors and some "plastic surgery" is a good place to start getting out of debt. —Wayne Coleman

Debt

Let no debt remain outstanding.
—St. Paul

Using credit is an easy way to obtain material goods, to have what we want, and have it today—not later.

We may begin by convincing ourselves we not only need, but also deserve and must have, whatever new or enticing item is being offered for just an "easy monthly payment." In this way, desires become needs, and, frequently, the only way to meet such desires is to rob from

tomorrow's income
by borrowing.

Golden Agers, especially those who have incurred excessive debt in the past, have learned that operating on a cash basis helps assure a more comfortable retirement. We can make wise choices about the items we need versus the items we want and let our desires be guided by our values, rather than the other way around.

As Charles Spurgeon said, "It is not how much we have, but how much we enjoy that makes happiness." Getting out of debt is a priority for those who would enjoy pressureless living during their Golden Years.

Nugget of Hope

Living within boundaries and limits is the only way to attain the highest and best success in our lives. —Cecil O. Kemp, Jr.

Budgeting

Budget giving first,
　　forced saving second,
and spending last.
　　　　　　—Cecil O. Kemp, Jr.

In his book *Wisdom & Money*, Cecil O. Kemp, Jr., says that priority on giving and saving is the first principle of wise budgeting. Wisdom teaches us to spend only the income left over after applying that wise principle and not to pad our spending capability by using debt to increase our cash flow. The best budgets lean toward giving, not borrowing, and toward spending moderation and efficiency.

We all want to reduce stress and anxiety and attain financial peace of mind in our Golden Years. Consider these wise ideas:

- First budget for giving, then for forced saving. (Forced saving is a system for automatically transferring money to savings accounts. "Out of sight, out of mind" money won't be spent. Forced saving helps assure there's gold in the Golden Years!)

- Spend when necessary, but resist using credit.

- Eliminate every possible debt. Use your income that is in excess of budgeted giving, saving, and spending to lower and completely pay off all existing debt.

Nugget of Hope
Empower giving and savings and take the power away from spending.
—Cecil O. Kemp, Jr.

Insurance

If anyone does not provide for his own family, he is worse than a h e a t h e n .
—*St. Paul*

Life insurance can help our loved ones survive financially after we die. We need enough life insurance coverage so that, together with our accumulated net assets, our families will have a stream of income to replace the income we provided.

There really is no quantitative rule of thumb to measure how much insurance each of us should carry; we must search our hearts to determine what we need to provide for our loved ones.

In addition to Medicare or employment-related medical insurance, most people will also need good supplementary medical insurance. Plan for enough to cover deductibles, co-payments, and non-covered items that your medical history indicates you may need. Examine your coverage carefully, so that you can resist sales pitches for insurance you don't need.

Although we can't plan away every risk, we can certainly prepare for the possible financial difficulties of illness and death. Our loved ones will appreciate our thoughtfulness.

Nugget of Hope

A legacy of unconditional love is more valuable and lasts far longer than a legacy of money and things.
—*Cecil O. Kemp, Jr.*

SOCIAL SECURITY

God has stored up ***great blessings*** *for those who trust and revere Him.*

—*King David*

The Social Security Act of 1936 was meant to supplement retirement income or savings. It was never intended to cover all expenses for retiring seniors. In fact, for most people, Social Security payouts fund only about one-third of their retirement income needs. Despite its limitations, Social Security is the sole means of economic survival for many older people who did not plan for retirement early enough—or at all, in some cases.

Wisdom teaches us to be accountable for our actions and responsible for ourselves and our families. We can welcome the responsibility of determining what our financial needs will be for retirement and then acting to fulfill them, according to our principles and values. In this way, we will be empowered to make wise choices for ourselves and our families. We can look forward in retirement to Real Security instead of Social Security.

Nugget of Hope

First, determine where you are and where you will need to be, financially. Then, bridge the gap by saving more, now.
—Cecil O. Kemp, Jr.

A Second Career

*They will still produce...*and be vital.
—*King David*

Financial adviser Larry Burkett wrote, "It would be very shortsighted for most people to assume they can earn as much at age seventy as they do at fifty, or that they will be able to live off Social Security. For some, it will mean a second career, after retirement." There are many reasons to consider a second career after retirement—most of which are positive and empowering.

The idea of a second career appeals to many of today's Golden Agers who still have ample vitality for some kind of active work. Physically, they continue to have a need for discipline and activity. Seniors who have enjoyed being with co-workers before retirement will probably continue to enjoy the companionship and teamwork of a second career. And, although additional income may be a welcome supplement to their budgets, many older people seek second careers for the joy of helping others, often on a volunteer basis.

We may not earn as much money at seventy as we do at fifty, but the rewards of a second career can outweigh the financial measures. We can reap a rich reward of love and companionship.

Nugget of Hope
Find a job you enjoy and you will never have to work.

Change of Lifestyle

Let your moderation be *known* to everyone.
—*St. Paul*

To live comfortably in your Golden Years takes long-range planning and preparation. Even then, some may still have to change their lifestyle in retirement. A long life may not be very happy if it is interrupted with financial stresses. Certain fixed expenses cannot be avoided but choice (discretionary) expenditures may have to be curtailed. For most who reach their Golden Years, necessary expenses are generally lower than at any other period of adult life. Yet, a change of lifestyle may still be necessary. Greet any changes with enthusiasm.

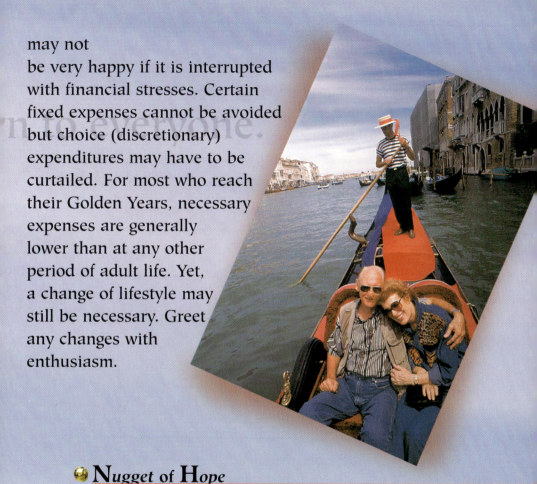

Nugget of Hope
It's so hard when I have to, and so easy when I want to.
—Sondra Anice Barnes

Home Mortgages

*It is required that we be responsible
for
whatever
is entrusted to us.*
—St. Paul

By the time most people reach their Golden Years, they will have fully paid their home mortgages. This home equity, in many cases, is the largest asset many older people will have.

Getting immediate cash or monthly income from home equity is normally a very, very unwise idea. There are many tempting opportunities to tap into home equity, such as trading down to a smaller house unnecessarily, or taking a reverse mortgage, a second mortgage, or a home equity loan. These avenues for raising cash can be expensive emotionally and financially, in the short run and the long run. Careful planning and budgeting can help older people keep their home equity intact and avoid the pitfalls of debt in their later years.

Oscar Wilde once said, "Experience is the name everyone gives their mistakes." Wise Golden Agers have learned from their abundant life experience to preserve their home equity.

Nugget of Hope
The peace of mind of having your home paid for is a valuable emotional asset that should not be sacrificed.
—Cecil O. Kemp, Jr.

Investments

Why didn't you put my money on deposit, so I could have **collected interest?**
—*A Parable by Jesus*

If you discipline yourself to practice good fiscal habits, you can turn a handful of dollars into much more and move in the direction of financial success and prosperity.

Cecil O. Kemp, Jr., in his book *Wisdom & Money*, has some good advice for us: "Regardless of age, our priority in investing should be return of capital, not return on capital. This means being conservative, but keeping enough growth assets in our investment mix to make sure we stay ahead of inflation and taxes. Many times a 'guaranteed' investment means a guaranteed loss. I call guaranteed investments

'Sticker Shock Investments.' That's because their owners get sticker shock when they realize their already low investment return, less taxes and inflation, often is no return at all and frequently translates to actual loss of principal. That's what I mean by guaranteed loss!"

Wise investors don't overexpose their capital to risk of loss of principal. And they know that the only guaranteed return comes from generosity of spirit and the giving of unconditional love!

Nugget of Hope
None can determine richness or poorness by turning to their asset and investment ledgers.
—Cecil O. Kemp, Jr.

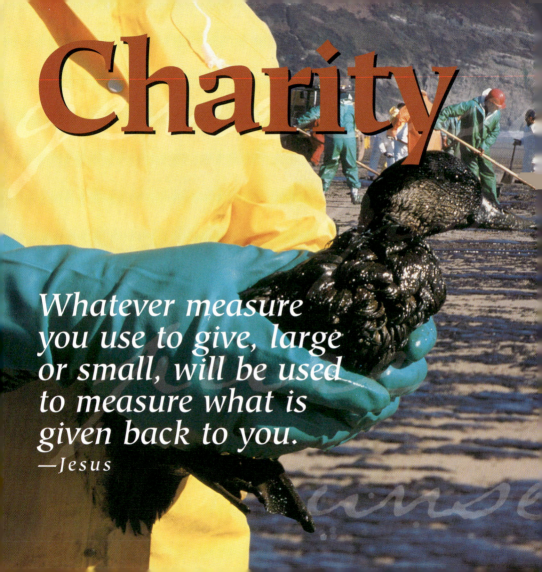

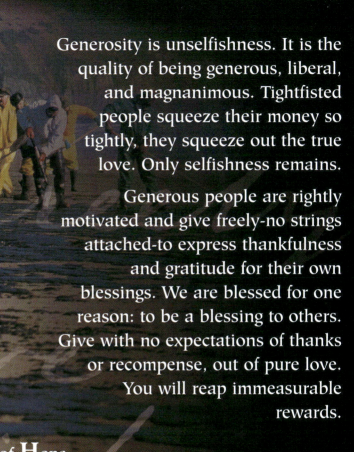

Generosity is unselfishness. It is the quality of being generous, liberal, and magnanimous. Tightfisted people squeeze their money so tightly, they squeeze out the true love. Only selfishness remains.

Generous people are rightly motivated and give freely-no strings attached-to express thankfulness and gratitude for their own blessings. We are blessed for one reason: to be a blessing to others. Give with no expectations of thanks or recompense, out of pure love. You will reap immeasurable rewards.

Nugget of Hope

Money never makes us happy...the more a person has the more they want. Instead of filling a vacuum, it makes one.
—Ben Franklin

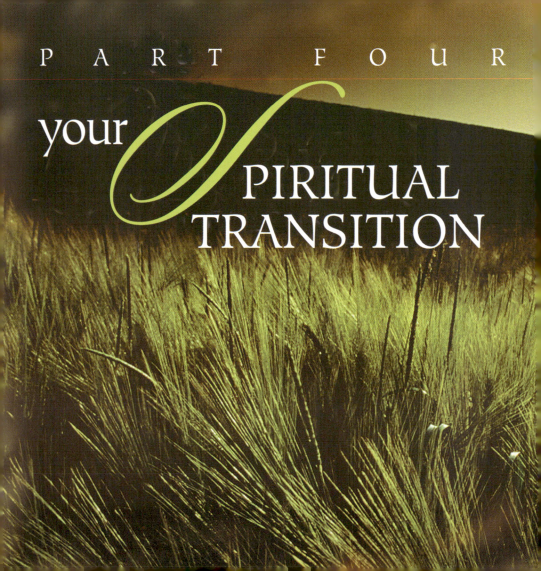

PART FOUR
your Spiritual Transition

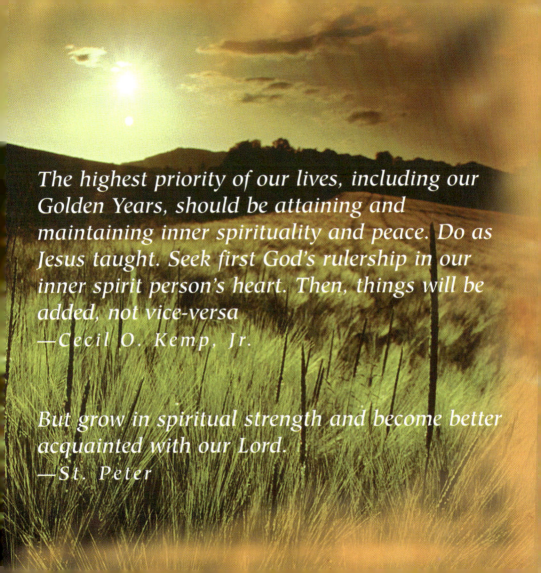

The highest priority of our lives, including our Golden Years, should be attaining and maintaining inner spirituality and peace. Do as Jesus taught. Seek first God's rulership in our inner spirit person's heart. Then, things will be added, not vice-versa
—Cecil O. Kemp, Jr.

But grow in spiritual strength and become better acquainted with our Lord.
—St. Peter

Prime Time Living

Give me time to tell this new generation (and their children too) about all your mighty miracles.
—King David

Most retired people have no time clocks to punch, no deadlines to meet, and fewer pressures to perform. If you choose not to have a second career, you are free to use your time where it is most valuable.

There are literally thousands of areas in the world where your knowledge and experience are needed. First, and most important, determine where God specifically wants you. When you find the right thing to do, in the right place, at the right time, God will bless you, and you will experience joy you have never known. That is real "prime time" living!

Nugget of Hope

Lord, make me an instrument of your peace.
—St. Francis of Assisi

Common Sense and Wisdom

*We have two lives. There's the one we learn
with and the one we live after that.*
—Bernard Malamud

To wisdom belongs intellectual apprehension of eternal things; to knowledge, the rational knowledge of temporary things.
—St. Augustine

Throughout your life you have accumulated much knowledge and a myriad of experiences. Over the years, as you have learned to make wise choices, your common sense has matured into wisdom. Now it is time to share your wisdom with others. As you give yourself to others and share the talents, common sense, and wisdom you have been blessed with, life will take on a new and fuller meaning.

Nugget of Hope
People are interested in how much we care, not how much we know.
—Cecil O. Kemp, Sr.

Leadership

And now go, lead the people to the place I told you about.
— *Moses*

Golden Agers have arrived at a natural place of leadership. They have acquired knowledge and experience and often have time to share their wisdom with others. The principles of Wisdom teach us that true leaders are true servants, who consider the needs of others above their own.

Assuming your place of leadership in your church, club, or community will bring far greater rewards than money. Helping others provides a sense of being needed, a natural component of healthy self-worth. Give the gift of your leadership and reap the rewards of your generosity.

Nugget of Hope
The welfare of each is bound up in the welfare of all.
—Helen Keller

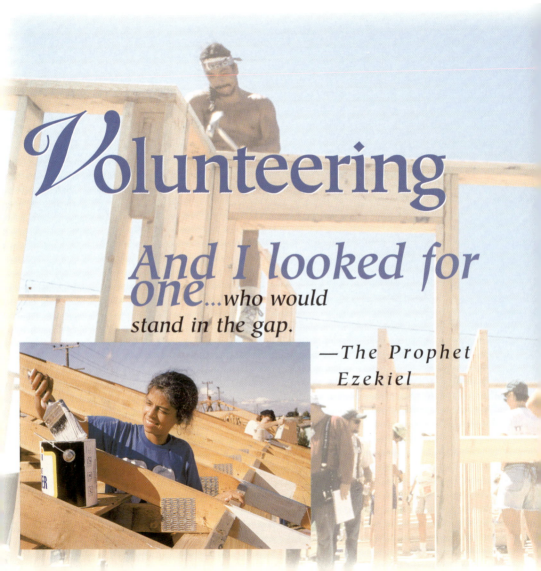

Volunteering

And I looked for one...who would stand in the gap.

—*The Prophet Ezekiel*

You have retired and no longer go to work every day. But you don't have to become a wallflower, waiting for someone to ask you to participate. You can take the first step and volunteer.

There are hundreds of places and thousands of people who could benefit from the gift of your time. Once you have determined where you might share your time and talents, volunteer for the job.

You can take responsibility by volunteering for clubs, organizations, or your church. Spend time with young people or with other retired people who need companionship. Help someone start a new business or teach someone to cook. Plant a neighborhood garden. Read a book for the Talking Library. You have a wise and willing spirit—you are ready to help!

Nugget of Hope

I do not intend to resign when I retire, but to re-sign to an appropriate ministry.
—Pastor David Larsen

Serving Others

Love each with affection.
Delight in honoring each other.
—St. Paul

In his book *Wisdom Honor & Hope*, Cecil O. Kemp, Jr., wrote this about Wisdom's Passion:

"Wisdom instructs the servant attitude is to be the attitude of our mind. St. Paul teaches us that we must not be selfish, nor live to make a good impression on others, but be humble, thinking of others as no less than ourselves. And we must not just think about our own affairs, but be keenly interested in others, so much so that we are motivated to attend to their best interests. This humble servant attitude is ready, willing, and able to prefer others before self.

Mother Teresa said, 'It's not how much we do, but how much love we put into doing.' She knew the truth of something George Bernard Shaw said: 'This is the true joy of life: Being used for a purpose recognized by yourself as a mighty one.'

Last, but not least, Antoine de Saint-Exupéry said, 'True love is inexhaustible: the more you give, the more you have. And if you draw from the true fountainhead, the more water you draw, the more abundant the flow.'"

Nugget of Hope

Leave a legacy of giving and sharing, yourself and your resources. Live and work by Wisdom's Motive, unconditional love, and Wisdom's Passion, serving others.
—*Cecil O. Kemp, Jr.*

Mentoring

Urge the young to behave carefully, taking life seriously.
—St. Paul

Lord, make me an instrument of Thy peace;

Where there is hatred, let me put love;

Where there is anger, let me put forgiveness;

Where there is discord, let me put unity;

Where there is doubt, let me put faith;

Where there is error, let me put truth;

Where there is despair, let me bring happiness;

Where there is sadness, let me bring joy;

Where there is darkness, let me bring light.

Nugget of Hope
Because it is in giving that we receive; In forgiving that we obtain forgiveness; In dying that we rise to eternal life.
—St. Francis of Assisi

Quiet Times

Do everything God wants, meditating on His laws and thinking about ways to follow Him more closely.
—St. Paul

S. C. Ainlay wrote that retired persons often find their personal relationship with God becomes more important to them. With maturity and the experience that comes from life's many blessings, their joy in the Lord becomes more personal and meaningful.

Bible reading and study become increasingly interesting. Prayer and meditation take on a new vitality. Perhaps retirees have more time-or perhaps they have learned to concentrate on what is important. Faith and hope grow together as people mature and apply the principles of Wisdom to this new and interesting stage of life.

Nugget of Hope
Wisdom is the only compass we need to guide us upward and remind us of our eternal purpose.
—Cecil O. Kemp, Jr.

Bible Study

Study to gain approval, to rightly discern the word of truth.

—St. Paul

Reading and studying are distinct. Studying involves meditation, deep thoughts about what has been read. Study is to reading as digestion is to food. To get the most nutrition from your food, your body must digest it. To get the most from Bible reading, you must "digest" what you read, using your heart and then your mind, to find your inner spiritual path.

You can find great joy in Bible study, if you go about it in a wise way. If you enjoy just reading the Bible, but have never studied the Bible closely, start by reading one chapter. Think about what you have read. Pray, and listen for God to talk to you. Meditate on God's Word, research what you have read, and read some more. Soon, Bible study will become an integral part of your life's journey.

Nugget of Hope
Wisdom and the Spirit of God inside us are the Perfect Union. —Cecil O. Kemp, Jr.

Knowing God

Perfect peace is the reward of the person whose mind is focused, totally concentrated on **God.**

—The Prophet Isaiah

Philosopher Blaise Pascal said, "It is the heart that experiences God, and not reason….The heart has reasons of which reason knows nothing." As we journey through life, God guides us in the ways of Wisdom, Honor, and Hope, and the Spirit of God grows within us.

You can have a closer relationship with God. Begin by developing the wise habit of daily Bible reading. Then add daily prayer. Third, make time for quiet meditation with God.

When you read the Bible, you will learn more about God's character and unconditional love. In prayer, you will have the opportunity to talk with God. In meditation, you listen for God to talk to you. God leads us toward a world of wonder and Truth.

Nugget of Hope

Prayer is an invisible tool that makes a visible difference.
In prayer, you talk; meditation is God's turn.
—Cecil O. Kemp, Jr.

Spiritual Gifts

I want to write about the special abilities the Spirit of God gives to each of you.
—St. Paul

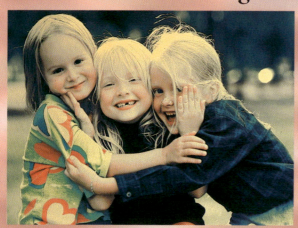

Every child of God has a spiritual gift, according to Bible teachings. Yet, many may not recognize their gifts, while others spend years trying to figure out how to use their gifts. Earl Nightingale spoke of that special journey we take in search of our gifts when he said, "Our first journey is to find that special place for us."

Spiritual gifts may be different from innate talents you may have had since your physical birth. It is important to determine your spiritual gift and put it into practice as you grow and become a vital part of God's Kingdom. Once you realize what your gift is, you can use it to serve others with passion and love.

Nugget of Hope
Allow yourself to discover what can be done when God gives your inner spirit person the graces of Wisdom, Honor, and Hope.
—*Debbie Guthery and Cecil O. Kemp, Jr.*

Bonding

A true friend is always loyal, and a brother is born to help in time of need.

— King Solomon

Every person needs a friend. That's why it is important to develop friendships with several people. Take the time and expend the effort to share your inmost thoughts, hurts, dreams, and secrets with someone you trust. A bond will soon develop between you.

You may find that you have a few friends whom you help, and a few other friends who help you. Bonding takes place when you share willingly with both kinds of friends.

These true bonds grow stronger and more fruitful with age.

◉ Nugget of Hope

Infinite sharing is the law of God's inner life.
—*Thomas Merton*

Balanced Life

Let everyone see that you are unselfish and considerate in all you do.
—St. Paul

Noted author and speaker Charles Swindoll wrote, "The right kind of toughness—strength of character—ought to mark the (person) of today." Tenderness and gentleness, outward qualities that demonstrate inner spiritual grace, are equally important.

God has placed balance on the list of nine qualities He feels

should mark the life of His children. Our goal is balance in our character, not just toughness. As Cecil O. Kemp, Jr., says in *Wisdom Honor & Hope*, "Adopt and always follow the Golden Rule of Wisdom. Love others as you love yourself. Defer, in your thoughts and behavior, to their best interests."

See how balanced your life can become when you live according to your heart's Wisdom?

Nugget of Hope
Today is the first day of the rest of your life.

ABOUT THE PUBLISHER

The Wisdom Company (TWC) began in 1983. Its founder, Cecil O. Kemp, Jr., grew up on a small rural farm and married his childhood sweetheart, Patty. Their two children have each made the Kemps doting Grandparents. Cecil graduated college in 1971, immediately passed the CPA exam, and worked with one of the world's largest accounting firms. He became Chief Financial Officer of a publicly held stock company at 23, and its COO before 30. Since 1982, the Kemps have owned many successful businesses, including TWC.

TWC's purpose is Sharing The Hope of Wisdom. Its inspirational and character education materials all express the principles, values, and priorities of spiritual Truth—as expressed in Cecil's acclaimed book, Wisdom Honor & Hope which points to The Inner Path to True Greatness. TWC offers two series of Collectible Gift Books, The Hope Collection and The Wisdom Series. Our aim in each book is to encourage the reader and to share:

- A renaissance of the individual lifestyle shaped by Wisdom
- The way toward true excellence and lasting success
- The Inner Path of integrity in daily living, thinking and decision making
- The joy of achieving and maintaining Inner Peace, the wellspring of true happiness and satisfaction